Alastair Frew is a partner in Lodders' Real Estate group. He heads up the Business Property Team and specialises in advising commercial property developers and investors.

A Practical Guide to Highway Issues in Property Transactions

A Practical Guide to Highway Issues in Property Transactions

Alastair Frew
Solicitor

Law Brief Publishing

Published 2020 by Law Brief Publishing, an imprint of Law Brief Publishing Ltd
30 The Parks
Minehead
Somerset
TA24 8BT

www.lawbriefpublishing.com

Paperback: 978-1-913715-15-1

PREFACE

The law of highways seems a little obscure and irrelevant. Don't we all just get in our cars and drive? But actually, there is so much more to it than that. This book is aimed at lawyers who want to get to grips with this subject but who don't really know where to start. Hopefully, this book should help you to answer your clients' key questions such as "what does a highway look like? Who can use one? How to you create one and who has to repair it afterwards?" and should point you in the right direction for further research.

Stand and deliver, your money or your life. Such was the cry of the highwayman during the 1700s, up and down the length and breadth of these islands. Highway robbery, nowadays just a reference to goods being over-priced, was a serious problem years ago. Violent robbers would terrorise travellers on the King's Highway, demanding that they came to a standstill, and hand over all of their goods. Happily, the last case of highway robbery was as long ago as the 1890s. Today, we seem to have replaced it with carjacking and street mugging.

The highway network is the lifeblood of the nation, for purposes good as well as nefarious. The highway was the Information Super-highway for thousands of years. There are well over 200,000 miles of tarmacked roads in the UK alone. The Romans laid their famous cobblestones over hundreds of miles of already ancient roads around southern Britain, as well as building many more. The Fosse Way, from Exeter to Lincoln, was laid by the Romans as the temporary north-western frontier of their Empire. Its name, rather unglamorously, just means "Ditch Road". The Salt Way running out of Droitwich in Worcestershire, before eventually crossing the Fosse Way, is of unknown antiquity but certainly pre-dates the Romans. Unsurprisingly, it was used to transport salt from Droitwich's famous brine springs, generations before the town became a bathing spa; perhaps the indigenous peoples of these islands were using it to trade salt right from the first days after the passing of the last Ice Age.

The Staffordshire Hoard of Anglo-Saxon treasures was discovered in 2009 near Lichfield, in a field next to Watling Street. That old road, now called the A5, runs from the English Channel up to Wroxeter in Shropshire. Fording the River Thames at Westminster, it is a Roman extension of an ancient Celtic road, which was then re-named by the Anglo-Saxons, the first speakers of our English language, after the regional capital of Wætlingaceaster (that St Albans to you and me). Legend has it that Dick Turpin, that most famous of highway robbers, frequented Watling Street.

Highways. Byways. Roads. Streets. Ways. Motorways. Cycleways. Bridleways. We use them all every time we leave the house, and they are always available for us, free to use and for use freely.

But, what is a highway? Is it the same as a street? Why do we have a highway authority, as well as a Streets Authority and a Traffic Authority? How does a road become a highway, and what happens if it doesn't?

Does any of it matter anyway?

The book is considered to be correct as at 1st October 2020.

My thanks should really be given to my two wonderful colleagues Michael Orlik (himself a published authority on this subject, and whose own book I have been very careful not to look at – although I did read it a few years ago) and Victoria Longmore (who now realises why I keep asking her obscure questions).

Alastair Frew
October 2020

CONTENTS

CHAPTER ONE
WHAT IS A HIGHWAY?

The answer to the question: what is a highway? is simple. A highway is a road.

When the Romans landed on these shores, they found an extensive network of roads, the product of the excellent surveyors of the ancient Celts. The Romans then re-engineered many of them with their famous cobblestones, and we now call those roads "Ways," from the Latin "Via" which means "road". In most of our villages, towns and cities, we have Anglo Saxon roads; a network of "Lanes", joined together by "Streets." A "lane" was once a narrow road, with hedges, while a "street" would usually have been paved or surfaced. The early English joined villages together with "Rides" which gives us our word "Road." They were to be wide enough to ride a horse along.

As passionate Europeans, we call our ring roads "Boulevards", named after the ramparts which once encircled Paris. We call our arterial roads "Avenues.", which traditionally run directly into the town centre ("avenir"/arrive, anyone?). As we will see later, an avenue is perhaps the archetypal highway – it takes you <u>to</u> somewhere.

In the middle of town, you might find a Square, even if someone has decided to call it a Place or a Plaza.

All of these types of road can be highways but might not be.

For thousands of years, the sole purpose of roads was to let people travel. Following the public health reforms of the Victorian period, roads started to be used also to provide a route for a network of sewers. Later, water pipes were laid, then gas, then electricity and more recently telecommunications fibres were all laid beneath our highways. Previously, any water or sewer pipes would just be put in the ground in nice straight lines, before the houses were constructed, and then built over. This is that reason that owners of mid-Victorian houses will often find a water main running under their living room. The subsequent use of the highway network for underground services seems to be much more logical, even if it does cause the odd headache when it comes to carrying out repairs to the pipework.

So, I have described what a highway is, without really defining it. As a lawyer, I should now give you the legal definition of a highway. The principal piece of legislation is the Highways Act 1980 (which I shall refer to simply as the Highways Act). In s328 of the Highways Act, a highway is defined as:

> *"the whole or part of the highway, other than a ferry or a waterway".*

As definitions go, this is not entirely helpful.

The word "highway" has been used for over 1,000 years, but these roads were "high" in the sense of Important, rather than "physically raised". Many writers point to the fact that highways were often raised up on embankments, but this is just a coincidence of good engineering combined with continual rebuilding over the centuries.

Under common law, any of Her Majesty's Subjects may pass and re-pass along a highway, as often and whenever they wish without let or hindrance and without charge. The use of the highway must be without time constraint and without toll or charge, although we will have to return to the issue of toll roads a little later.

The correct term for such a road is "highway". As lawyers, we should not use the term "public highway" as this just describes a highway which can be used by the public, and all highways can be used by the public. The use of the term "public" is probably a confused reference to the "adopted" status of the road.

Sometimes, we find a highway that is described as "private", which is generally a reference to it being unadopted. More on "adoption" shortly.

A highway must go from some place to another place. A highway must serve some purpose. As lawyers, we say that a highway must have "utility". This is why an avenue is an archetypal highway, as it runs directly to something. A private avenue might run to a grand country house, while a highway avenue might run to a town centre. That said, a cul-de-sac <u>can</u> be a highway and many thousands of them are highways. More recently, highway authorities have started to deny adopted highway status to many modern culs-de-sac. (See references to the Manual for Streets in "What is the Adoptable Standard?" below).

The law does not define the Anglo-Saxon word "road". It has been in common usage for more than 1500 years, and everyone knows what a road is. It is only lawyers who turn to a book to find a definition of the word "road".

The law does give a definition of sorts for "street," which our Anglo-Saxon ancestors would have known as a road with a paved surface, a word they took from the Romans, with their paved "strata." In the New Roads and Street Works Act 1991, we see "street" defined as a "highway, road, lane, footway, alley or passage, square or court and any land laid out as a way whether it is for the time being formed as a way or not." There is an apparent contradiction in this; linguistically, a street must be paved but the law allows for a road that has not been laid out yet to be a street. The point is, it must be intended to be laid out. A street must be intended to be a street!

In other words, most of these crucial terms are not properly defined anywhere in statute.

Even though a "highway" is not clearly defined, it is an offence to obstruct a highway.

While the public have the right to use any highway, this does not include a right to roam or meander around. Strictly speaking, you must keep moving – standing still on a highway can bring you to the attention of the local Constable.

In the 19th Century case of Hickman v Maisey, Mr Maisey was prosecuted for standing on the highway in order to watch racehorses train at Newmarket.

Conversely, the 1999 House of Lords case of DDP v Jones and others, took a different view. A group of people who stood in peaceful protest at the side of the A344 at Stonehenge, objecting to the modern restrictions on access to the ancient stones, were held not to have committed an offence, even though they were quite obviously causing something of an obstruction.

The distinction between these two cases is explained by Lord Hutton in his judgment in the DDP v Jones, when he quoted from Halsbury's Laws of England:

> *"the right to pass along a highway for the purpose of legitimate travel; not to be on it, except so far as the public's presence is attributable to a reasonable and proper use of the highway as such. A person who is found using the highway for other purposes must be presumed to have gone there for those purposes and not with a legitimate object..."*

The protesters in Jones were engaged in a peaceful assembly with a legitimate purpose – they wanted to be able to access Stonehenge without having to pay for an entry ticket. Their assembly on the highway was therefore lawful, so the moderate obstruction they caused was lawful.

By contrast Mr Maisey had been standing on the highway in order to spy on Mr Hickman's racehorses, under training at Newmarket. Mr Maisey's purpose had been nefarious, so his moderate obstruction of the highway was unlawful. It brings to mind the recent "spying" scandal in professional football, where employees of Leeds United Football Club were found to have been standing on the highway while secretly watching rival teams' training sessions. This was found to have been in contravention of competition rules, but had this occurred 125 years ago, prosecutions may well have followed.

CHAPTER TWO
WHO CAN USE A HIGHWAY

Given that any of Her Majesty's Subjects may pass and re-pass along a highway, as often and whenever they wish without let or hindrance and without charge, it should be the case that anyone can use any highway at any time. Oh, that life were so simple.

Until the invention of motorised transport, it was true that all highways were available to all users, albeit some highways were too narrow or too steep for even the hardiest horse and cart driver.

As soon as we had cars, and to a lesser extent the steam traction engines that preceded them, we started to have distinctions between types of highway.

Nowadays, there is quite a list:

i. highways just for pedestrians

ii. highways for all persons including wheeled traffic;

iii. highways for pedestrians, bicycles, horses, cattle and sheep;

iv. highways for wheeled vehicles, where horses, pedestrians and cyclists are prohibited – these are Special Roads, such as motorways;

v. highways where Her Majesty's Subjects can be charged for access. These are Concession Roads – toll roads – such as the Birmingham North Relief Road (known as the M6 Toll).

Highways Just For Pedestrians

This category can easily be split in two:

Footpath – this is a highway which may only be used by pedestrians, and which is separate from a vehicular carriageway;

Footway – this is part of a highway, but which cannot be driven along by vehicles. Typically, this is the pavement or verge at the side of the road. While it is generally illegal to drive on a footway, nothing is ever quite that straightforward, and will look at the thorny issues of parking on the pavement and accessing your own driveway, a little later on.

Highways for all persons including wheeled traffic

This is your standard road. Almost all roads are open to all traffic, albeit they are often subject to various local prohibitions such as bus-only or cycle-only lanes, or perhaps maximum weight restrictions.

Highways for pedestrians, bicycles, horses, cattle and sheep

The ancient bridleway, as the name suggests, was open to horses as well as pedestrians. They are also open to cattle and sheep, and it is permitted to ride a bicycle along a bridleway. Occasionally, a new stretch of highway will be opened that is specifically open to pedestrians, cycles and horses, such as the bridge over the A38 at Weeford in North Warwickshire.

You may come across the term "drove road" or "driffold". These are the remnants of the ancient seasonal roads that were used for driving (we might say, herding) cattle from one pasture to another. Ancient drove roads are often quite easily identified out in the countryside, as they are fairly narrow roads with generous green verges, but with a stone wall on either side; perfect for herding hungry cattle, who could snack on the verges as they walked along. Typically, such drove roads are now highways open to all traffic, rather than just pedestrians and animals. They are often unadopted, and therefore somewhat difficult to pass along.

Special Roads

After several thousand years, our road network was suddenly expected to cope with the new-fangled invention of the high-speed motor car. Our road network was not able to cope, so a new network was planned and built for the first time – the motorways. Pedestrians are prohibited, as are low powered vehicles, on the very obvious grounds of safety.

Concession Roads

Once the motorway network had been built, the nation still needed more roads. Our appetite for travel seems to be insatiable. The Government of the day decided that the next motorway to be built should pay for itself, just as the bridges over our main river estuaries have had to. From this decision was born the Birmingham North Relief Road, commonly known as the M6 Toll. It is a highway, but by Act of Parliament a toll may be charged. Unlike other highways, if you don't pay, you cannot use it.

The problem of Bicycles

I am a keen cyclist, but I don't cycle on the pavement (footway) because it is dangerous. It is also illegal. Young children may cycle on the footway, but adults cannot although a blind eye may often be turned to an adult carefully accompanying a child.

Cyclists may use bridleways but have no public right to use footpaths. There is much confusion surrounding this, because many hundreds of miles of footpath are also cycleways, but this just means that the stretch of path has been given two designations – highway (footpath) and also private right or easement open to a class of users (permissory cycleway).

Recently, special cycle tracks have been introduced, where cyclists are permitted and have right of way. There are also "shared space" designations, where cyclists must ride on one side while pedestrians must walk on the other.

Mobility vehicles

Common sense applies to the rights of mobility vehicle users; they may use footpaths and footways and are allowed to use the carriageway of all roads apart from Special Roads. Driving a mobility scooter on a motorway is not a good idea.

Highways and Private Rights

Just as a footpath may be used by cyclists if an additional permission has been granted, so any highway might also be the subject of additional private rights.

For example, anyone walking along a public footpath (which is a highway) as it crosses a farmyard, would be well advised to look out for heavy lorries driving along the path. While it is illegal to drive along a footpath, it is perfectly lawful to do so if the owner of the path has granted a private right. Perhaps the farmer owns some commercial units, which have been let out to a haulage company. Perhaps, the farm is so long established, that various neighbours have prescriptive easements over the farmyard for gaining access to their homes which pre-date the highway designation. In each case, that would allow vehicles to be driven lawfully along a public footpath. A private right can exist alongside the public right of highway.

In the same way, the owner of a pedestrian shopping precinct will usually allow commercial delivery vehicles to drive across the pedestrian areas at certain times of day, even though some of the precinct will be highway, designated for pedestrian traffic only.

Village Greens and Common Land

A village green may also be a highway. This is can cause confusion, as it is unlawful to drive on a village green, but it is lawful to drive on a highway. The green in question may have been designated as highway at some point in the past, and in such cases the green itself may have been nibbled away by highway improvements until there is very little left to see.

By contrast, a highway may not cross common land. It is illegal to drive on common land – although as with public footpaths, it is open to the owner of the common to grant private rights. Therefore, frontagers are able to acquire prescriptive rights to drive over a common.

Furthermore, in direct contradiction to the paragraph above, many commons <u>are</u> crossed by highways. This is a relic from times past; it is no longer possible to designate a road which crosses a common as a highway.

The legal position has seesawed over the last few decades.

The Law of Property Act 1925 s193 made it illegal to drive a vehicle on common land, and s34 of the Road Traffic Act 1988 prohibited anyone from driving a vehicle in order to access the owner's home, if the distance was less than 15 metres. Long distance travel over common land could be permitted by the common owner, but for short distances, the homeowners were expected to park up and walk.

Lawyers used to assume that if someone had openly driven over the land for 20 years without asking for permission and without using force, then they would have established a prescriptive easement. Then in the early 1990s, the Court of Appeal handed down its judgment in the case of Hanning v Top Deck Travel [1993] 68 P&CR 14. This judgment turned the law on its head; prescriptive easements were not possible, as the act of driving on a common was illegal. The owners of various commons, often local authorities, started asking homeowners to pay considerable sums of money to be allowed to carry on driving to their homes.

The law was in a muddle and needed to be changed.

At the turn of the century, the Countryside and Rights of Way Act 2000 was enacted, and s68 attempted to address this problem. A statutory framework for purchasing an easement from an unwilling common owner was created. Payments of 10% of the value of the home had been demanded, but the new framework limited this to a range of 0.25% - 2% of the value of the property.

While very welcome, this framework was not quite good enough, and has now been repealed.

In 2004, the House of Lords, in the case of Bakewell Management Ltd v Brandwood and others (www.bailii.org/uk/cases/UKHL/2004/14.html) finally overruled the judgement in the Hanning case and held that it was after all possible to obtain a prescriptive easement over common land.

Common sense has prevailed, and homeowners who had been driving to their homes for a generation or more could continue to do so without being held to ransom. Any new easements that might be required are left to open market negotiation.

As for driving across a village green, where it is not also a highway, an important point was made by the Court of Appeal in Massey and Drew v Boulden [EWCA Civ 2002 1634].

The Court held that it was possible to obtain a prescriptive vehicular easement over a registered village green. In this particular case, the Court noted that the user did not injure the village green or cause any material interruption to its wider use and enjoyment. In any event, the prescriptive use predated the registration of the green, so this case may simply be authority for the wider principle that land can be given two use classes at once – some land is pedestrian-only highway, while also having private vehicular easements over it, while in Massey v Bouldon, the land became a "car free village green" while already subject to established (if unclaimed) vehicular rights.

What about Bridges?

Bridges are another special case. If a bridge carries a highway, the bridge is usually (but not always) also a highway.

However, it is perfectly possible for a privately-owned bridge to carry an adopted highway. There are hundreds of old bridges, constructed as part of the canal and railway networks, and then sold off as surplus to requirements by the railway and canal operators. Such bridges are now privately owned.

If the bridge is physically part of the highway, but the structure remains in private ownership, then the duty to maintain the bridge includes the next 300 feet of carriageway on either side of the bridge structure. This can impose a significant burden on the owners of old bridges, which were built for horse and cart traffic but now carry motorised traffic.

In 1999, the laden weight limit for lorries was increased from 38 tonnes to 44 tonnes, on the basis that new lorries have more axles, so there was no increase in weight loading. Many old bridges were simply not designed for this extra weight, and private bridge owners were entitled to ask the highway authority to upgrade the structure of any bridge that had not been designed to carry more than 24 tonnes.

In many cases, the highway authority declined to pay for the engineering works but instead imposed weight or speed limits over these old bridges. This has led to a plethora of road signage on country lanes. Given how regularly the speed limit is ignored, one wonders how often these weight limits are discretely ignored as well, causing our old bridges slowly to buckle under the force of the traffic passing over them? It remains the case that old bridges typically collapse under the force of flood water rather than heavy traffic, but it is nonetheless an area for concern. In February 2020, the RAC Foundation Bridge Maintenance survey indicated that more than 3,000 bridges in the UK were substandard, being incapable of safely carrying a 44tonne lorry. While there are more than 70,000 publicly owned bridges in this country, as well as many privately-owned ones, this figure of 3,000 is still somewhat alarming.

CHAPTER THREE
WHO DECIDES WHO CAN USE THE HIGHWAY?

We have seen that, broadly, anyone can use a highway. That is after all the point of a highway, being a road open to all of Her Majesty's Subjects. We have also seen that nothing is quite so simple.

The use of a highway is *regulated* by the Traffic Authority. This applies to all highways, whether adopted or unadopted.

The Traffic Authority is typically the same body as the highway authority, which is responsible for the maintenance of adopted highways and for keeping unadopted highways open for safe use. The statutory function of the Traffic Authority is to regulate the use of all highways. In order to do this the Traffic Authority can impose restrictions on parking or usage of any highway. It can impose Traffic Regulation Orders, introducing taxi lanes, bus lane or cycle lanes. It can introduce local speed limits, construct speed humps, paint yellow lines and prohibit parking.

This power extends to all highways. We have not yet discussed the term "adoption" but the Traffic Authority has power whether the highway is adopted or not.

Crucially, it can also impose restrictions on parking or usage of <u>any road commonly used</u> by the public.

As we saw above, the word "road" is not defined in law. We all know what a road looks like when we see one. Also, the term "public" is not defined. The Public is the "public generally", and however loosely defined this is, we all know what it means.

This is of huge importance, as it means that the Traffic Authority has the ability to impose restrictions on any stretch of road that is open to the public at large. For example, a hospital carpark will have been built for the public to use when visiting a public building. Equally, a supermarket carpark will have been built for use by the public at large. By contrast, the carpark to a small office block will have been built only with the staff and customers of that business in mind, and not the general public.

From this, it follows that the Traffic Authority has power to regulate the use of a supermarket car park.

The white lines in most car parks were painted by the owners, and the speed limit signs in a hospital car park are generally just private signs without legally binding force, but the rules of the road still apply.

If you disobey the private signage, you are not guilty of speeding. However, is you are driving dangerously, you can still be prosecuted for your dangerous driving, even if it takes place on a supermarket car park.

CHAPTER FOUR
HOW DO YOU CREATE A HIGHWAY?

A highway is created when a road or footpath is "dedicated" by the landowner to the public for use as a highway, and the public accepts that dedication. In addition, the road must be useful to the public – lawyers use the phrase "it must have utility."

As will come as no surprise to readers of this book, there is no single procedure for the process of "dedication."

Traditionally, use by the public for a period of more than 20 years would be evidence that the road should become highway, provided that the public could prove that the landowner had intended to dedicate the road as a highway. This is similar to the requirement for the creation of a prescriptive easement, but the user of the road is by the public at large, rather than just a specific individual or owner of a particular property. In other words, if one person can claim 20 years' user, then she or he is not entitled to claim that the road is a highway but could claim a personal easement by prescription.

The twenty year period is not set in stone; in the case of Rachel Young v Merthyr Tydfil Council in 2009, a period of just four years was sufficient. This was a case involving a footpath over Council land, which was held to have been dedicated after just four years' user, although it had not been adopted. It can be distinguished from other cases on the grounds on public policy, as it was a personal injury case, where Ms Young tripped and fell on the unadopted footpath.

If the landowner co-operates by accepting that the road was indeed intended to be a highway, then after 20 yeas' user by the public, the road would be deemed dedicated.

However, if the landowner refused to co-operate, what could the public do about it?

The answer is simple – as with the example above of a personal prescriptive easement, if the public at large can prove their use was "as of right" without interruption from the landowner, then this is deemed to be dedication by the landowner and acceptance by the public.

Remember that use "by right" is entirely different to use "as of right." If the public use the road without permission but acting as if they had been given permission, they are acting "as of right." After twenty years' user as of right, the public can claim that the highway has been dedicated.

By contrast, if the landowner grants permission, then the use can be said to be "by right", that is with permission. Such use by the public cannot result in the creation of a highway.

By way of example, the postman bringing letters to my front door uses my driveway "by right", with my permission.

A further example would be a landowner who locked the gates on his or her road for one day each year. The following day, the gate is unlocked, and the public are allowed in. The use by the public on those 364 days was therefore by right/with permission rather than as of right.

This was discussed by the House of Lords in the 2007 case of R (on the application of Godmanchester Town Council) v Secretary of

State for the Environment, Food and Rural Affairs (and others) [2007] UKHL 28.

In the Godmanchester case, the landowner failed to persuade the House of Lords that it had not intended to dedicate its footpath as a highway, so the footpath was held to have been dedicated as a highway.

The landowner was a local town council, which had written to the county council in its capacity as highway authority, to notify it that the footpath in question was not intended to be a highway. The town council however failed to erect any notices on the land. It had therefore served a formal notice on the highway authority but had not thought to tell the public at large. Following user by the public without the town council's permission, the road was held to be a highway.

As something of an aside, the Court considered that the landowner should have communicated with the public and might have been better served by erecting a gate. However, a gate is only effective if it actually stops people from gaining access. When gate posts are erected, there is often a small gap, and this can quickly become a large gap if the gate fills a gap in a hedge, as determined members of the public start squeezing through that gap. A gate might keep vehicles out, thereby preventing the road from becoming a vehicular highway, but the road might instead be declared to have been dedicated as a pedestrian highway - a public footpath.

Allowing members of the public to claim rights of highway over a road simply by twenty years' user was becoming increasingly troublesome, as various special interest groups spent time researching old "lost lanes" and then taking action to have them dedicated as highways.

As a result, in October 2013, the Highways Act 1980 was amended to give landowners a way of defeating the 20-year rule.

Any landowner could submit to the highway authority a "landowner statement" under section 31(6) of the Highways Act. This is a declaration that certain specified roads and paths on the landowner's estate had been dedicated for use by the public, and therefore that the remaining roads and paths had not been so dedicated. The purpose of the s31(6) statement was to bring clarity and so to reduce the growing tensions between countryside walkers and farming landowners.

Section 31(6) wisely adds the caveat that the lodging of such a statement will only be effective "in the absence of proof of a contrary intention." A landowner cannot create a nice new footpath, generously surface it, and leave it wholly ungated without expecting members of the public to start using it. Simply to rely on a s31(6) statement to prevent a claim of rights of highway in such a case would be unwise.

In any event, individuals can still use the 20year rule in order to claim an easement for the benefit of a specific plot of land. Sometimes the evidence which is brought in support of a claim for a new highway is held by the Court to be inadequate but is still sufficient for the grant of a private easement. It largely depends on how many people have been using the road, and what land that road can be said to benefit. (Please see Loder v Gaden, below).

Very importantly, if a landowner uses the s31(6) statement to confirm dedication of a road as a highway, this does not place any obligation on the highway authority to adopt it. In practice, the s31(6) statement tends to be used to confirm that there are No Highways crossing the land, rather than to declare new highways.

The Right to Roam and Lost Lanes

But, what about the Right to Roam? The law in England and Wales regarding rights of access to the countryside was significantly changed with the introduction of the Countryside and Rights of Way Act 2000, in order to narrow the gap with Scottish law, which since ancient times has granted to the public a much wider set of rights. The public at large can now walk on land defined as "access land", being generally open land in hill country. Unless the landowner grants additional permission, the right to roam does not apply to horse-riding, cycling or driving any vehicle other than a mobility scooter or powered wheelchair. It is a right to use open land. It is a right to roam about, to meander. As we discussed at the outset of this book, a right of highway does not give anyone the right to meander about, but only to pass and re-pass.

A right to roam therefore does not give anyone a right of highway. It does not rise to a presumption that the land has been dedicated as a highway.

Following on from this change in the law, another change was required. As mentioned above, "lost lanes" were being "discovered" by campaign groups with the inevitable arguments over their status as highways.

The Natural Environment and Rural Communities Act 2006 (NERC 2006) introduced restrictions on the dedication and adoption of highways and prevented the informal adoption of vehicular highways.

Section 66(1) of NERC 2006 states:

> *S66 (1) No public right of way for mechanically propelled vehicles is created after commencement unless it is—*

(a) created (by an enactment or instrument or otherwise) on terms that expressly provide for it to be a right of way for such vehicles, or

(b) created by the construction, in exercise of powers conferred by virtue of any enactment, of a road intended to be used by such vehicles.

(2) For the purposes of the creation after commencement of any other public right of way, use (whenever occurring) of a way by mechanically propelled vehicles is to be disregarded.

In other words, following its introduction, the dedication of an existing vehicular highway must be in writing, while any newly constructed road will only become a vehicular highway if that process is in accordance with other legislation (such as s38 Highways Act, which we will come on to shortly).

NERC 2006 also provided that ancient vehicular highways that were not shown on any Highway authority definitive map or any landowner statement would now cease to be vehicular highways. The "lost lanes" lobby had been given ample opportunity to open up these old roads, but the door was now being closed.

If an ancient road is not listed as a vehicular highway, it can now only become such a highway with the express written consent of the landowner.

But not all highways; the changes brought by NERC 2006 only apply to vehicular highways, or to quote from the Act, ways used by mechanically propelled vehicles. This new law does not apply to footpaths.

In February 2012, the Country Land and Business Association published The Right Way Forward, its report on rural rights of way.

This CLA report stated: "It is wholly wrong, and defies all sense of propriety and logic, that paths which have been unused for decades, centuries or even at all, can be 'discovered' out of the blue and opened up across land … when there has been no use within living memory and there is no evidence of a path on the ground." The CLA, which campaigns on behalf of substantial parts of the rural landowning economy, remains concerned that other campaign groups are still trying (presumably, successfully) to uncover old "lost lanes" across land owned by its members. The CLA's position is supported by a certain logic, but Parliament has not seen fit to lend its support. It is certainly true that "lost lane-ing" is a popular past time, for City dwellers like your author, seeking to escape the noise of town by using the road less travelled.

Not every highway must be Dedicated

There is one exception to the rule that a highway must be dedicated. This is where the highway authority itself has purchased land for the purpose of laying out a highway. Therefore, motorways and modern trunk roads are highways without ever having been dedicated, as are many local roads serving public facilities developed by the local council.

Dedication is not Adoption

It is important to remember that "dedication" does not affect the ownership of the road or the soil beneath it. Dedication merely creates a right for all of Her Majesty's Subjects to use the road as a highway, and this includes the soil down to two spades' depth.

Two Spits Deep

This rule of "two spades/spits' depth" was a dictum of Lord Denning in the Court of Appeal case of Tithe Redemption Commission v Runcorn Urban District Council [1954] Ch 383. Lord Denning being Lord Denning, his dicta tended to carry more weight than perhaps even he intended.

In fact, the highway is as deep as it needs to be; a trunk road with mains services and a large storm drain beneath it will be significantly deeper. The highway also extends upwards, as far as is necessary, typically 20 feet. In major city centres, the precise vertical extent of the highway is extremely contentious, as it has an impact on the ability to create metro systems and sell "flying" advertising space.

This issue is of great significance if the land is itself highly valuable.

In London, there are huge swathes of land which are now vested in Transport for London, having previously been owned by the former Greater London Authority. These parcels comprise, amongst others, highway land. The problem is that huge swathes of land also passed from the Greater London Authority into the hands of the various different London Boroughs. As much of that land is extremely valuable, it's ownership can be hotly contested.

Transport for London should only be holding the land required for its purposes, but how much land it that? How much land vested in TfL?

In the Supreme Court case of London Borough of Southwark and another v Transport for London [2018] UKSC 63, Southwark argued for a narrow definition, using Lord Denning's famous "two spits" maxim. Applying this upwards and outwards, Southwark felt that TfL should only have control over the carriageway itself. Southwark wanted ownership of the airspace above the highway, while leaving the road (plus, presumably, the height of a double decker bus) to TfL.

This would have given Southwark the valuable higher airspace, often wanted by developers for the oversailing of cranes during construction works. The Highways Act 1980 (s177) requires that anyone wishing to use the airspace over a highway must obtain the licence of the highway authority. This is an income stream which Southwark wanted to be able to claim as residuary landowner, rather than seeing it all go to TfL as highway authority.

However, the Supreme Court did not support Southwark. Seeking to replace once and for all Lord Denning's "two spits", Lord Briggs referred instead to the "zone of ordinary use." He left this phrase deliciously vague, as is the way with all things Highway.

The upshot of the Southwark case is that TfL's freehold portfolio now includes land to the side of the carriageway, and all the airspace which would be within the zone of ordinary use. In a high-rise city, that would seem to include everything up to the top of the highest tower crane.

The land comprising the highway remains the property of the landowner, subject to the rights of the public to use the surface and the rights of statutory utility companies to lay their equipment beneath (or above and beside) the highway.

CHAPTER FIVE
WHO MAINTAINS THE HIGHWAY?

When a highway develops a pothole, whose responsibility is it to fill it in?

The short answer is that the highway authority is responsible for filling in those potholes, and for all maintenance of any highway, if that highway is adopted as maintainable at the public expense.

Under s41 of the Highways Act 1980, the highway authority has a duty to maintain an adopted highway unless it can show that someone else should have the responsibility.

This leads to an obvious question – who is the highway authority?

The answer varies, depending on the type of highway. I summarise the situation as follows:

- Trunk roads and motorways – the Secretary of State for Transport

- Highways in London – Transport for London

- Highways in Metropolitan Boroughs or Unitary Authorities – the relevant metropolitan authority

- All other adopted highways in England – the County Council

- Highways in Wales – the County Borough Council.

While the duty falls to the Highway authority, which for the majority of the country will be the County Council, this duty is often sub-contracted to the local district council. The actual repair works may then be carried out by a private contractor, whose vans may bear a slogan such as "working in partnership with Stratford on Avon District Council on behalf of Warwickshire Highways".

The relevant highway authority is required to keep a register of all highways within its maintenance obligation. This should include:

- all highways that existed before 31 August 1835;
- all public footpaths that have existed since 16th December 1949;
- all highways built for the public by the highway authority; and
- all highways adopted since 31st August 1835.

The date of 31st August 1835 was the date on which the Highways Act 1835 was enacted. This was an important piece of modernising legislation, which recognised the need for the regular maintenance of the highways network for the good of the nation as a whole. As an interesting aside, the Highways Act 1835 also introduced the obligation on the owners of all waggons, and consequently all modern lorries, to paint their name and address legibly on the right-hand side of the vehicle!

The duty to maintain a highway must be carried out in all circumstances, however extreme.

If the road stood on a causeway or embankment which was part of the highway, and that embankment collapses or is washed away in a storm, then strictly speaking the highway authority must rebuild the causeway or embankment and then reinstate the road, regardless of the expense, even if that requires it to rebuild the causeway or embankment.

If a sea wall is breached, allowing the storm waters to carry away a highway, then arguably the highway authority must repair the sea wall and then reinstate the highway. The difficult point here is that if the land on which the road stands is washed out into the sea, then that strip of land has legally ceased to exist, and the highway has necessarily also ceased to exist. At that point, the duty to maintain also ceases. If a "natural" coastline is destroyed by the sea, then the highway authority is not required to reinstate any highway which is lost with it, but if a coastal embankment is destroyed then the highway authority will have a duty to repair.

The duty of highway maintenance includes the obligation to clear snow and mud from the carriageway and footway. We are all used to seeing snow ploughs deployed by the highway authority to clear snow, or more usually to spread grit and salt to prevent the formation of ice, but I have never seen any highway authority contractors clearing mud off the highway. It is now common to see signs at the exit points from major building sites, reminding the drivers of construction vehicles that they must not carry mud onto the highway, and I regularly see signs warning of "mud of the road", but I have never witnessed the highway authority actually carrying out its duty to clear this mud.

This can be something of a problem, when combined with the heavier rainfall patterns which we are currently experiencing, as large amounts of soil are washed onto rural roads each winter.

More about highway drainage a little later.

In the event of a failure to maintain, including any problems with ice or mud, then the highway authority is liable for any personal injury or damage caused by such failure.

In 2017, the High Court considered the case of Paul Singh v City of Cardiff Council (2017 EWHC 1499). Mr Singh was walking home from the pub one dark winter's evening, when he stepped off a footpath at the start of a footbridge. Having left the footpath, which was unfenced, he slipped and fell down a steep bank and into the cold waters of the Llanishen Brook in the northern suburbs of the city of Cardiff. He suffered very serious injuries.

Despite the obvious risks, the Court held that the Council was not responsible for Mr Singh's injuries. The footpath had been reasonably maintained, so the Council had discharged its responsibility. The Court held that Mr Singh had fallen because he had stepped off the path; he had not fallen on the path itself. Mr Singh's very argument was that he had fallen off the footpath because it had not been properly fenced. The Court took great care to investigate whether or not the Council had a duty to fence the path, so as to protect members of the public from suffering as Mr Singh had done. The Court held that there was no such duty; it would have been tantamount to requiring all footpaths to be enclosed with security fencing. Therefore, the Court found in favour of the highway authority.

The Singh case related to an adopted footpath, being part of a network of urban footpaths under the care of Cardiff City Council.

Unadopted public footpaths are common. Indeed, most of Britain's 140,000 miles of footpaths and bridleways are unadopted. Typically, these will be sign-posted as public footpaths crossing open countryside or farmland, without any form of made surface. No hard surface is ever laid, and no maintenance of the surface is ever carried out, unless the landowner happens to want to install land drains etc for his or her wider purposes.

Private, or unadopted as we should now say, vehicular highways are fairly rare. However, if a landowner takes the step of dedicating a road as a highway without ensuring that this highway is adopted as maintainable at the public expense, then that landowner must maintain the highway.

The owner of an unadopted highway can require the highway authority to adopt that road, by following the procedure set out in Section 53 of the Highways Act 1980. If a landowner considers that is no longer wishes to maintain an unadopted highway which crosses its land, then that owner can bring a complaint before the Magistrates Court, requiring that the road be adopted. The highway authority is entitled to object, on the basis that the road is not of sufficient utility for the public. At trial, the Magistrate will then settle the issue, and may order the that highway be adopted, provided that the landowner pays a suitable lump sum to the highway authority to cover the cost of future maintenances. As we have discussed already, the landowner would be best advised to discuss matters with the highway authority and to agree a suitable programme of works and the level of the required financial contribution. Taking the Council to Court remains a useful, if expensive, option if negotiations break down.

The payment of the financial contribution is also likely to be expensive, but it does at least have the merit of bringing the landowner's liability for ongoing maintenance to an end.

Alternatively, if the private road has not been dedicated as a highway, but is frequently used by the public, the landowners may prefer to preserve the undedicated status of the road and charge members of the public a toll for its use. For instance, there is a bridge which links the A493 with the A496 at Penmaenpool/Llynpenmaen on the southern edge of Snowdonia, in Wales. This Grade II listed structure is privately owned, and each of the 1,000 or more vehicles to cross it each week are charged a toll by the owners. While the A493 and A496 are most certainly highways adopted as maintainable at the public expense, this popular toll bridge remains private, unadopted and is not-dedicated as a highway. The owners could close it if they wished.

The Clifton Suspension Bridge near Bristol is a classic example of a toll bridge. The bridge itself was built by a private company and remains privately owned, but it carries an adopted highway, the B3129. The toll charged is used to keep the carriageway, as well as the famous bridge itself, in good repair, as perhaps to reduce traffic flow across the elderly structure.

Toll highways (whether roads, bridges or tunnels) are rare, but far from unknown.

The Birmingham North Relief Road, better known as the M6 Toll, was the first modern road in this country to be built with the intention that it would be a highway for which a toll would be charged. An Act of Parliament was required for this, as it was contrary to the common law rule that Her Majesty's Subjects should be able to pass and repass along a highway free from charge.

Toll tunnels are a much more common part of the UK highway network; while tunnels are fairly rare, many of them have a toll-charge in place. For instance, you will be charged a toll for using the Mersey Queensway Tunnel in between Liverpool and Birkenhead. If you use the Thames tunnel crossings between Dartford and Thurrock, you will discover that a toll is charged.

In 2018, toll charges were ended on the older of the two Severn Bridges, because the various tolls collected had equalled the amount laid down in the original Act of Parliament, for the construction and maintenance of the bridge. The toll to use the Dartford Tunnel was to have been scrapped in 2003, as the tolls raised had fully paid for the cost of the constructions works, which were funded by the taxpayer. However, in an attempt to dampen demand to use the tunnels, the toll remains firmly in place. This is against the spirit of the imposition of tolls on highways, as they were intended to be cost neutral.

What happens if the road is maintainable by no one?

There are a large number of older housing estates across the UK where the roads have become highways due unrestricted public user for a period of more than 20 years, but without any formal dedication ever having taken place. If they post-date the 1957 threshold discussed below, such roads would automatically be highways. If they pre-date 1957, but the 20year test has been passed, they are also deemed to have been dedicated as highways.

Unfortunately, if a pre-1957 Council estate road has not been formally dedicated by the subsoil owner, typically the local housing authority, then there can have been no adoption, leaving the duty to maintain unclear.

In these cases, the local highway authority does not have the right to maintain the roads, although as we discuss a little later, if the housing authority is the same as the highway authority, then the council can and must maintain the roads.

There is a power for the highway authority to "step in" and take over the road, but only if it is clear that there is a landowner who is "to blame". Not every local authority which has fallen behind with its road repairs can be said to be "to blame".

We must turn once again to the Highways Act. The highway authority has a duty under s130 and s230 of the Highways Act 1980 to carry out repairs in order to "obviate dangers to traffic", such as the filling in of potholes and carrying out of other emergency repairs. This duty requires the carrying out of works in order to prevent damage to vehicles and/or harm to road users. It does not allow the highway authority to carry out any strategic repairs, or any upgrading. Furthermore, as we have seen several times already, all such repair works are to be re-charged to the landowners, who would typically be the local district council or perhaps a housing association or even the individual frontagers.

Disputes can be settled in the Magistrates Court, who can order that the highway authority must adopt the estate roads. Once again, the sting in the tail is that the cost bringing the road up to an adoptable standard must be paid by the frontagers.

In addition to this duty to obviate dangers to traffic, the highway authority is required by s333 of the Highways Act to protect the public from nuisance. In a well-publicised case in 2001, the London Borough of Wandsworth successfully sued Railtrack for the cost of abating the nuisance caused by pigeon droppings, which were falling from nesting sites on a railway bridge and making the footway dangerously slippery. The duty to keep the footway safe to walk along fell to the London Borough, as highway authority, which was being put to unnecessary expense by the railway company's unwillingness to tackle to problem of pigeons roosting on its bridges over the footway. The Court held that Railtrack was liable to reimburse Wandsworth for such expenses.

Can anyone repair a highway?

The simple answer is that only the highway authority can carry out repairs to an adopted highway.

Of course, if the highway is unadopted, the position is different. As we have seen, unadopted highways are most commonly rural footpaths or bridleways, where the highway authority has the duty to ensure that the way is kept open for the public under section 130 of the Highways Act but is not responsible for maintenance.

Turning back to adopted highways, it is an offence to carry out works to the highway without the express consent of the highway authority.

While it may be uncommon for anyone to carry out repairs to a public road – most will simply send an email to the Council – property developers and construction companies regularly need to carry out works on the highway. Every time a new road or entrance drive is built, in order to connect it to the highway network the structure of the carriageway must be cut into, so that the engineering of the junction is sound. Larger developments might require a roundabout, or an extra traffic lane. These features are likely to require the existing carriageway to be widened, in turn requiring the footways to be relocated.

All such works require the consent of the highway authority.

If the road works are considered to be of benefit to the public, the highway authority will give its consent but only if the developer and the owners of all affected land enter into a formal deed of agreement with the highway authority before works can begin.

The document looks rather like the section 38 agreement discussed below but will typically be carried out under section 278 of the

Highways Act, which authorises works to be carried out to an existing highway. The highway authority is entitled to perform the works, although if this is the county council, then it will often grant permission back to the developer to carry out the improvements itself, subject to suitable monitoring by the authority's highways engineers.

If the highway works require additional land, such as in the case of a new roundabout or the various accommodating works, landscaping or footways, then the developer must provide the necessary space, with the owner(s) of the additional land joining into the required deed. Such a document would be entered into under both section 278 and also section 38 of the Highways Act. This is because works are being carried out to an existing highway, and road workings are taking place on further land which will be dedicated as highway and adopted as maintainable at the public expense.

Do these rules apply to private home-owners?

At the other end of the scale, a private home-owner may wish to construct a driveway into his or her house, crossing the existing footway. There is a common law right to drive a vehicle across the footway, so it may be possible for a home-owner simply to turn off the carriageway and drive straight onto his or her private property. However, it is an offence to drive on the footway if it endangers pedestrians although an attentive driver need not be troubled by this. However, it is also an offence to bring mud onto the highway or to cause damage to the footway. It is therefore potentially unlawful to drive a car from your front lawn onto the highway. It is almost certainly unlawful to do so if you have to bump up and down the kerb to get between your land and the carriageway.

To avoid such problems, the home-owner must lay a proper driveway, with a hard surface. The home-owner must also dig up and then re-lay the footway with a stronger foundation; footways are built to an engineering standard that makes then safe to carry the weight of pedestrians, but they are not engineered to carry the weight of moving vehicles.

The homeowner must therefore have the formal consent of the highway authority. In urban settings, the county council as highway authority will typically agree to grant licence for a footway crossing provided that the homeowner pays for the necessary engineering works to ensure that the footway is properly strengthened and lowered. The licence will be a very simple document and will refer to section 184 of the Highways. Most s184 licence documents will also require the driveway to the dwelling house to be properly constructed, in order to avoid mud or gravel being carried onto the footway, where it can cause a nuisance to pedestrians or damage to the surface of the footway itself. Any gravel driveway should be constructed so that there is a deep lip or cill, with the gravel bed being several inches below the level of the footway, in order to stop gravel being carried out and onto the highway. Despite this, we probably all have neighbours with incorrectly constructed gravel driveways, with gravel being spread up and down the street, pressed into (and causing damage to) the tarmac, and clogging up the storm drains.

For anyone who lives in a more rural setting, or adjacent to a trunk road, the process may be more complicated if the highway engineer feels that a simple driveway is not safe due to the speed of the passing traffic. In such cases, a "visibility splay" or "turning head" must be provided to allow vehicles driving along the trunk road ample time to see any car attempting to turn out of the private drive. If the home-owner is lucky enough to own a wide tract of frontage land, then a suitable area can be re-laid as the visibility splay. Otherwise, it may be that the existing highway verge is sufficient to accommodate the splay. Either way, an agreement under s278 and possibly s38 will be required, just as with a commercial development.

A word about unadopted highways

Who is responsible for maintaining a road which is unadopted highway, or a road which is not a highway at all? In each case, the answer is the freeholder of the land over which the highway runs. If the road is not a highway, then any maintenance obligation will be a private matter between the owner and any persons with a right to use the road. However, if the road is an unadopted highway, the subsoil owner must keep it in repair such that the highway users may safely pass and repass over it.

The highway authority has no duty to carry out maintenance to unadopted highways, and actually has no right to do so, subject to the following caveat:

If an unadopted vehicular highway has become a danger to traffic, the highway authority has a duty to ensure that it is repaired. Section 230 of the Highways Act 1980 states that the highway authority must require that the owner of the highway carries out repairs. If they are not carried out, then the highway authority must carry out repairs in order to "obviate dangers to traffic", such as the filling in of pot-holes and carrying out of other emergency repairs. The costs are then charged back to the owners/frontagers. This process often leads to the frontagers applying to have the road adopted as maintainable at the public expense under one of the procedures described above.

If the unadopted highway is a footpath, the landowner has no duty to maintain the road, provided that he or she does not cause damage to it. This principle has applied to highways since a court ruling in the year 1446 and for many centuries it applied to all forms of highway. Following the increase in vehicular traffic and in particular the development of motorised traffic, this ancient principal has been gradually narrowed in scope. The historic exemption still applies to unadopted public footpaths but unadopted vehicular highways must now be maintained by the owner of the highway subsoil.

CHAPTER SIX
WHAT IS "ADOPTION" AND HOW DO YOU DO IT?

So far in this book, I have used the term "adoption" on a number of occasions, without telling you what it means. If dedication is the process whereby a road becomes a highway, what is "adoption"?

Adoption is the process whereby the public takes over responsibility for maintaining and repairing the highway from the landowner. If a highway is not adopted, the landowner remains responsible for maintaining and repairing it. The "public" in this instance is the highway authority, which has the statutory duty to maintain adopted highways, at the public expense. A significant part of our local and national taxation goes to the maintenance of the highways which we, as Subjects of Her Majesty, are entitled to pass along without charge. There used to be a specific road tax, paid by car owners for the maintenance of the adopted highway network. This tax was abolished in 1937 at the instigation of a certain Winston Churchill. Since then our highways have been maintained out of general taxation.

Given that maintenance of a highway can be very costly, it follows that a road owner is unlikely to wish to dedicate it to the public use as a highway unless the public agrees to pay for its maintenance and repair. To put it another way, why would you dedicate your road as a highway unless the highway authority agrees in advance to adopt the road as a highway maintainable at the public expense.

A road which is dedicated but not adopted is an unadopted highway, being a "private road" which anyone can use, but which the landowner must maintain. This is not usually the desired position.

As the process of adoption involves a public authority, there are various procedures specified and one or other of them must be followed.

Section 38 Highways Act

The is the most commonly used procedure is set out in section 38 of the Highways Act.

If a developer is building houses, it will usually also need to build roads. Very often, the house builder will want the local highway authority to take over the responsibility for maintaining these roads into the future. Once the houses are built, the developer can sell the units and then walk away from the site leaving future road maintenance to the highway authority. In return, the highway authority benefits from a portion of the Council tax raised from the new homes.

As we will discuss later, not all new housing estate roads are intended to be highways. Some housing estates are branded as being rather upmarket and are tucked away behind gates. In other cases, the main estate roads will become highways, while various shorter spur roads leading to the houses themselves will stay as private roads. As you might imagine, this situation regularly leads to disputes between house builders and highway authorities, although it remains the case that the majority of new roads being built are still adopted by the local highway authority.

In order to ensure that a new road is adopted under the procedure set out in s38 Highways Act, the landowner (strictly, it is the landowner, not the developer) will typically enter into a written agreement with the highway authority to do the following:

i. To build the road;

ii. To dedicate the road as a highway. The road is now a highway, but maintainable by the developer;

iii. To maintain the road for a period of 12 months once it has been completed. This is the "maintenance period"; and

iv. To pay a financial contribution to the highway authority or provide a financial Bond. This is usually the subject of extensive negotiations, as the developer will want to preserve its cash reserves, while the authority will want to ensure that sufficient funds are deposited, or secured by an institutional bond, to cover the cost of any works. This leads to further debates about exactly what works the money is intended to cover, and for how long.

In return for these specific contractual commitments, the highway authority contracts with the landowner that, once all this has been done, it will adopt the highway as maintainable at the public expense once the landowner has fulfilled its obligations.

For obvious reasons, s38 agreements generally are also signed by the housebuilder/developer, or execution is delayed until the developer has become the landowner.

In the list set out above, you will see that the landowner/developer must carry out various works but also must make a payment, either in cash or by way of a bond. The purpose for this is to ensure that the highway authority has the money to finish off the road in the event that the developer fails to do so or becomes insolvent before the works are completed.

However, in 2014 the world of the "Section 38 Bond payment" was rather badly shaken.

In R (on the application of Redrow Homes Ltd v Knowsley Metropolitan Borough Council) (2014 EWCA Civ 1433), the Court of Appeal held that the highway authority was entitled to require the developer to pay future maintenance costs post-adoption of the highway.

Redrow had taken Knowsley Council to court over its demand for £39,000 for the future maintenance of street lighting. This is a fairly small sum of money to result in such costly litigation, but the developer clearly wanted to settle the wider principal, that the s38 payment was only to be used for pre-completion costs.

Unfortunately for the housebuilder, the Court of Appeal held that there was nothing in the language of the Highways Act 1980, s 38(6) which drew a distinction between what was permitted in respect of the period before and the period after the road became a highway maintainable at the public expense. The relevant section reads as follows:

> *Highways Act s38(6):*
>
> *An agreement under this section may contain such provisions as to the dedication as a highway of any road or way to which the agreement relates, the bearing of the expenses of the construction, maintenance or improvement of any highway, road, bridge or viaduct to which the agreement relates and other relevant matters as the authority making the agreement think fit.*

The authority can choose whether to fund the maintenance expenses itself, or to require the developer to pay for them. The judgment of the Court of Appeal in Redrow v Knowsley means that section 38 agreements for the adoption of highways may lawfully contain provisions for a payment (often referred to as a "commuted sum") to cover all aspects of future maintenance of the highway into the indefinite future, or a provision that the developer will itself pay for (or even carry out) all aspects of future maintenance whenever they become necessary.

The upshot of this decision has not been a dramatic inflation of s38 bond payments. Rather, housebuilders and local highway authorities are now embroiled in even more detailed negotiations as to what is payable and what is not, what is adoptable and what is not. More detail, more negotiation, and perhaps more delay.

S38 Agreements are personal

Agreements made under Section 38 Highways Act are personal to the original parties, and do not bind its successors. This can be a problem, if the developer sells the estate before the adoption has been completed. It is also quite common for a developer to obtain planning permission for a large scheme, together with the associated s38 Agreement, before selling parts of the site to third party house-builders. These buyers will not be bound by the terms of the s38 Agreement.

For this reason, many highway authorities require that their Section 38 agreements also refer to Section 106 of the Town and Country Planning Act 1990, which is intended to ensure that the agreement "runs with the land" and therefore binds successors.

It is arguable however that s106 TCPA is not an appropriate statutory provision for this purpose, as it refers to agreements entered into with the local planning authority rather than the local highway authority. Getting both of these bodies to execute the document is one additional problem for the developer, in addition to the widely held opinion that it is simply an incorrect use of the TCPA 1990.

As an alternative, some developers will offer a contractual obligation to any housebuilder who purchases part of the wider site, and also to their own plot buyers, that they will procure adoption of the road. A chain of private contracts can therefore build up, alongside the statutory s38 Agreement.

Problems with s38 Agreements

One problem of Section 38 agreements is that they rely on the developer and the highway authority agreeing that the road is properly built.

If you buy a house on a modern estate, you will probably have a legal easement to get to and from your property. For the reason we will see later, this easement may be expressed to operate until the road is adopted or it may be silent on this point. Either way, no problem – you have an easement allowing you to get to and from your house.

However, if the road is never properly finished to the exacting standards of the highway authority's engineering department, then the road will not become adopted. In such a case, who will maintain it? The housebuilder may have finished work, sold all the houses and been dissolved.

The highway authority will have access to the commuted sum, or the security bond, but the amount of this was generally only ever intended to be enough to allow the council to finish off a newly built road (subject of course to arguments following the Redrow case mentioned above).

The commuted sum might not be enough to allow the substantial reconstruction of a fairly old road that was never finished properly in the first place. Such a road might now be in a state of partial decay. This is far from uncommon; there are many housing estates where the estate road was built and finished to the satisfaction of the house-builder, but not to the satisfaction of the highway authority. The road was therefore not adopted. It may have been dedicated, but possibly by a company that has now been dissolved.

In such a scenario, the highway authority could step in, and finish the works. It would then claim the commuted sum, before calculating the shortfall and sending a bill to each householder!

In the scenario where the housebuilder is still in business, it might try to avoid this outcome by using the procedure set out in s37 of the Highways Act, as discussed below.

In the good old days, housing development schemes tended to include a nondescript spur road, leading to a gate or fence, with open land beyond. This was to enable a second phase of development to be carried out, which connect into the highway network through this spur road.

However, the local planning authority is less likely to permit such a spur road these days, and the highway authority may well object to such a planning application as statutory consultee. The expansion of the highway network by stealth is now frowned upon, but you will still see "phase two spur roads" on many existing housing developments, many of which are now being utilised for in-fill developments.

Section 37 Highways Act

In cases where there is no section 38 agreement, or where there is a dispute as to the interpretation of that agreement, the landowner can give notice to the highway authority under section 37 Highways Act, requiring the highway authority to adopt the highway.

If the council objects, the matter can be settled at trial in the Magistrates Court.

During the trial, the Stipendiary Magistrate will visit the site, and ask searching questions of the various engineers about any deficiencies which he or she notices in the standard or works.

The question to be decided is –

"Will the highway be of sufficient utility to the public to justify its being maintained at the public expense?"

The task for the housebuilder is to persuade the Magistrate that the road serves the required purpose (that word "utility" again) and that it was properly built, and that any issues with the road are simply a matter of maintenance. Conversely, the highway authority will seek to argue either that the road has insufficient utility to be a highway at all, or that it was not properly built.

Once this question has been settled by the Court, the newly dedicated highway still needs to be properly constructed. This involves technical argument.

If it has been properly constructed, it must then be opened for use as a highway and maintained for a period of 12 months. This can be difficult for the developer; the road has almost certainly been completed by this stage and proving the standard of construction might require digging up sections of the road in order to show to the highway authority's engineers that the foundations were properly laid!

Using Section 37 is therefore something of a blunt instrument. Often, it is used as a device to force the parties to come together for a detailed negotiation. Unfortunately, highway authority engineering departments can be so badly understaffed, that the only way to get a high-level technical meeting with the engineer is to force the matter to trial. The various engineers meet at Court and often are able to come up with a sensible compromise, allowing the formal proceedings to be settled without requiring a judgment from the Magistrate. A very blunt instrument, but sometimes an effective, if expensive, way to force a settlement of a dispute under Section 38.

Section 228 Highways Act

A highway authority can insist that a street becomes a highway maintainable at the public expense.

The owners of the street (who will be assumed to be the frontagers, if the owner of the street itself is unknown) can object, because they are required to pay for the cost of making the street up to adoptable standards. The trial is heard in the Magistrates Court.

However, Section 228 Highways Act can be a useful tool for a developer seeking to have an existing road adopted as part of new development works, where the owner of the road is not known.

If a development site fronts onto an existing private road, in unknown ownership, then the developer will become a "frontager" upon purchasing the development plot. The old maxim of Ad Medium Filum applies – unless there is evidence to the contrary, if you own land adjoining a highway, you also own up to the midpoint of that highway.

As one of the frontage owners, the developer can use the procedure in s228 Highways Act to force the highway authority to adopt the road.

The cost of the works will fall to the frontagers, but if the developer agrees to indemnify the other frontagers there may be no objections from them.

The developer must carry out the works, and then put up a notice on the site following completion of the works stating that the road is to become a highway maintainable at the public expense. Unless objections are received, the road becomes a highway maintainable at the public expense after just one month.

Objections are likely to come from the highway authority itself, if there is any question as to the standard of works. In any event, the highway authority can charge inspection fees, and will be able to raise technical questions regarding the standard of construction. A wise developer is therefore best advised to involve the highway authority throughout the process.

It is common for one or more of the other frontagers does object, perhaps on the grounds that they prefer the road to remain private so it can periodically be gated or because they have not been given a sufficient indemnity by the developer. If this happens, the highway authority will refer the matter to the Magistrates Court for trial.

As with s37 Highways Act, any road which is adopted under s228 must be of sufficient utility to the public and must be properly constructed.

Advance Payments Code

Do you want the roads to be adopted highways, or to remain private estate roads? Regardless, be aware of the Advance Payments Code, under which the highway authority can request money before any works can commence.

Authorised by sections 219-225 of the Highways Act, unless an agreement has been entered into under s38 Highways Act, the highway authority is entitled to serve an Advance Payments Code notice upon the landowner. Once development plans have been approved, the highway authority may serve an APC notice requiring payments to be made. The liability falls on the landowner rather than the developer, so a property owner will need to ensure that it has a suitable contract with its development partner.

The landowner (or its developer, as its agent) must lodge its estate layout plans for new building works including an unmade street, and the highway authority is entitled to require payment for the cost of making up that street to adoptable standards. This applies even if the street is not intended to become a highway, but to remain a private road.

The point of the Advance Payments Code is that almost all roads ultimately connect to the highway network and are used by members of the public. A private road that falls into decay will eventually become a danger to the public and therefore a liability on the public purse. For this reason, a landowner who is laying out the private road should pay money into the highways kitty to cover the costs of future maintenance.

Once an APC notice is served by the highway authority, the payment is compulsory.

A landowner must give notice to the highway authority of intention to commence and house building work on any property which connects to a highway, and failure to do so is an offence.

The highway authority then has six weeks to serve the APC notice on the landowner, notifying it of the sum required. This money is to be deposited by the owner with the highway authority and is used as security for the cost of works in instances where the highway authority carries out a private street works scheme, following a failure by the developer.

Once the new road has been properly constructed, the owner can apply for any surplus bond money to be refunded. It is a matter of contract between the original landowner, housebuilder and the purchasers of the new homes what should happen to this money. If the Advance Payments Code sum was paid by the housebuilder as landowner, then it is simple enough – the money is returned to the housebuilder who keeps it. However, if the houses are built on land not in the ownership of the housebuilder, but the Code sum is paid by the housebuilder, then the development agreement should address this issue. Also, if all the houses are built and sold before the Code payment is returned, the housebuilder will want to ensure that the Code sum is not returned to the homeowners, who will by then be "the owner".

The Advance Payments Code applies even when the street is not being dedicated as a highway but will remain as a private estate road. In such cases, the highway authority can grant an exemption, under s219 of the Highways Act, if it believes that the road is not likely to fall into such a state of disrepair that the highway authority would need to step in to repair it. For instance, this may occur if the road is just a short stretch of paving, being effectively a driveway shared by a small number of luxury dwellings.

Once a road has been released from the Code, the highway authority retains its statutory power to repair roads which are dangerous, or which are causing a hazard to the highway, but it cannot re-charge the cost of such works to the frontagers as would normally be the case when private street works are carried out by the highway authority. The highway authority will therefore only grant such an exemption if it is satisfied that the private road will be properly built and diligently maintained into the future.

Any grants of exemption should be registered as a local land charge, and discoverable on a local authority search. Any purchaser of a house, seeing such a charge, will know that the road is unadopted, that no Code sum has been deposited for its future repair but also that the highway authority will not be entitled to demand payments from the frontages. It may follow from this that the highway authority is unlikely to carry out future works, other than emergency repairs where the road has become a hazard. Such frontagers will therefore have to repair the road themselves. Properly drafted conveyancing documents will address this, with a chain or estate covenants or perhaps a management company.

The Advance Payments Code does not apply to industrial developments.

Roads built by the Department of Transport, or by highway authority for public use

If the highway authority builds a road for the public to use, then such a road is automatically a highway maintainable at the public expense, under s36(2)(a) Highways Act 1980.

A typical example would be a road linking the main highway to a public swimming bath. Unless it was obviously intended to be a gated road that was locked each night, this will be a highway.

Such highways are not always shown on conveyancing searches, which can provide difficulties for conveyancers. This can cause apparent anomalies in highways search results, with stretches of "unadopted" road linking together stretches of adopted highway. As we have seen, the "unadopted gap" may well be adopted by virtue of s36(2) Highways Act, without appearing as such on a search plan.

Council estate roads

As mentioned above, since 1957 any road within a council-built housing estate is automatically an adopted highway, but only if it has been properly built.

This leaves significant scope for argument between the local housing authority and local highway authority, on the question of engineering, as a road built in e.g. 1960 is unlikely to be in good repair now, even if it had been properly constructed.

The parties in such a dispute are often the district council and the county council respectively. However, the Courts have decided that in the case of unitary authorities, the different internal departments are not entitled to have this argument so the road must be treated as adopted.

What is the Adoptable Standard?

The Manual for Streets, as referred to earlier, is a lengthy guide published by the Department of Communities and Local Government, the Welsh Assembly Government and the Department of Transport. First published in 2007, it was intended to ensure that residential streets are designed with pedestrians and cyclists in mind, as well as motorists.

The Manual provides the basis for the design and construction specification of highways in England and Wales.

For those of you who appreciate the finer differences between the design requirements of local roads, collector roads and arterial roads, it is well worth a read. Perhaps more pertinently, it discusses the importance of controlling motorised traffic on a very local level. In modern housing estates, space is very much at a premium so not all roads, particularly side roads and the spurs leading off them, will have both a carriageway and a footway. Instead, they have a "shared surface highway" where both cars and pedestrians must share the same strip of tarmac.

The design issues discussed in the Manual for Streets become very important situations where a developer is at odds with the local highway authority over whether or not a road is to be adopted as maintainable at the public expense. If a housebuilder lays out a shared surface road, intending it to become an adopted highway, but the council declares that it is not of sufficient utility to the public to be worthy of adoption, the parties will quickly turn to the Manual for guidance. The highway authority might argue that the road does not serve enough houses, for instance if a local road has a park on one side, at the insistence of the local planning authority, even though the road in question links together two roads which will become adopted highways. Very small culs-de-sac are regularly refused by the highway authority. Serving just a few houses, they are arguably not really part of a public highway network, so many housebuilders will avoid going to the trouble of seeking adoption and will pass the road into the ownership of the frontagers by way of a management company. A larger cul-de-sac, with more houses, is more likely to prompt a dispute between house builder and highway authority, particularly if the road has been built to "adoptable standard".

Just for completeness, there is also the equally fascinating but less well-read Design Manual for Roads and Bridges. This is very much a technical document, dealing with issues such as whether or not a new highway bridge might cause a river to "scour", causing the bank to collapse and bringing flooding issues downstream. More prosaically, it discusses the engineering requirements of highway footways and the type of surface materials which should be used for cycle ways.

Unless the guidance in these Manuals is followed, the highway authority may well refuse to adopt the new road.

Unfortunately, but entirely typically of all things highway-related, the Manual is not an exhaustive specification. It is a book of guidance, rather than a rule book; developers will still need to agree design and construction specifications with the highway authority on a case by case basis. Otherwise, the parties will soon enough be looking up the provisions of s37 of the Highways Act.

CHAPTER SEVEN
HOW WIDE IS A HIGHWAY?

A pattern is emerging. Statute law is very little help in settling the question of how wide a highway should be.

The Public Health Act 1925 imposes a minimum width of 36 feet, but this is a measurement for the benefit of public health. If the gap between houses is more than 36 feet wide, there is no statute to decide how wide the highway should be.

Nowadays, the planning process takes a very close interest in this point, and planning authorities are required to follow the guidance offered by documents such as the Manual for Streets. Despite this, there is no national standard. There is no set specification which planning authorities, highway authorities and house builders are all required to use, setting out exactly how wide each type of highway should be.

While it is generally obvious that the carriageway and any paved footway is part of the highway, what about soft verges?

If cables and services are laid under the soft verge, under powers granted to the utility company by wayleave from the owner, then the verges are deemed to be private, and therefore not highway.

By contrast, if the statutory utility companies did not seek the permission of the landowner, then it is assumed that they operated under their statutory powers, which only apply to highways. These verges will be deemed to be highway.

For this reason, landowners who are selling land to developers will be asked to look through their boxes of old deeds very carefully, and to reply accurately to those Pre-Contract Enquiries. Did Grandfather sign a wayleave with the Postmaster General for those telephone cables which run along the farm boundary? Is there a dusty old document executed by Aunt Mabel which gave permission for the Town Corporation to lay a gas pipe? If so, then this is evidence that the land where the utility cables and pipes run is not part of the highway. If not, then the land may be presumed to be highway, unless the document has been lost. The utility companies have all been privatised, and old records have often been lost. Who keeps bank statements to prove that a wayleave payment of a few shillings a year was paid in the 1950s?

Fences

Fences are used to secure property. Fences keep trespassers out and/or animals (or children!) in. The location of fences should not be taken to mark the boundaries of a plot of land. In a suburban context, most people have a fence to mark their legal boundaries to the rear, but the front garden or driveway might be entirely unfenced. If there is a front lawn, it might extend right up to the highway verge, such that there is no immediately obvious delineation between garden lawn and highway verge.

The owner of a roadside restaurant might fence part of the beer garden, to make it safe for families, while leaving the carpark and parts of the garden open to the highway in order to attract passing trade.

In 2018, the Court of Appeal heard a very interesting case about a fence. (Annetts v Adeleye [2108] 1 WLR 4539). This was a dispute between two neighbours in an exclusive residential street in Sevenoaks in Kent. The conveyancing was complicated, with land changing hands on more than one occasion, but the basic point as issue was: if you put a fence across a right of way, does that stop it from being a right of way? In other words, does the erection of a fence result in the way being abandoned? The High Court accepted that the way had been abandoned, but the Court of Appeal overturned this, and re-established the long held principal that a way, once created, cannot be lost.

The Annetts case related to a private right of way rather than a highway, but the principal is the same. The Adeleye fence was put up to keep the family children safe inside their garden and was neither a boundary marker nor a permanent obstruction to the pre-existing easement. Once the fence was taken down, the full width of the easement was available for use, despite Ms Annetts' objection.

Equally, in the countryside, or alongside brownfield development plots, the location of a fence neither confirms the legal boundary nor the extent of the highway.

The fence is therefore a security feature, not a way of delineating the highway. Landowners sometimes erect fences simply to secure certain parts of their property, rather than to mark out the exact boundaries.

Despite this, the initial assumption remains that a fence in the near vicinity of a highway is intended to mark the boundary of the highway. It is up to the landowner to prove otherwise. If the landowner can produce evidence that the fence-line was created for a purpose other than the delineation of an ownership boundary (taking "ownership" to be land free from the right of highway), particularly if the disputed unfenced strip has been maintained over the years by the landowner rather than by the highway authority, then the Court will typically take a common sense approach.

Hedges and ditches

Don't get caught in the trap of the "hedge and ditch rule".

If the highway is next to a ditch which is itself next to a hedge, and the hedge and ditch also form part of an ancient field boundary, then it is assumed that neither the hedge nor the ditch are part of the highway, but that they are both part of the neighbouring field. This is the "hedge and ditch presumption". It is not a "rule".

The thinking goes that, in days gone by, in order to create a robust boundary feature, you would first dig a drainage ditch and then you would throw the soil up to form a mound alongside the ditch. Along the top of this mound, you would plant a thorn hedge, which would by now be an ancient hedgerow.

All of these works must have taken place on "your" land, so the owner of the ancient hedge is presumed also to own the drainage ditch. But, this is a presumption and not a rule, and it only applies if the hedge in question was originally a boundary marker, rather than merely a way of sub-dividing a larger estate. To prove this, will require some research into ancient maps and conveyancing documents.

If the hedge and ditch are modern, then this assumption does not apply in any event.

Either way, if the highway authority wants to claim ownership of a ditch, then it must prove that the hedge forms the boundary of the highway, and therefore that the ditch is part of the highway. Alternatively, it must prove that the hedge and the ditch were established entirely separately.

Sensibly, if the ditch was dug by the highway authority, effectively as a highway storm drain, then it is assumed that the ditch is part of the highway. The adjacent landowner might be able to produce documents to counter this presumption, in the form of a highway drainage agreement which would suggest that the ditch was dug on land outside the highway itself. Generally, the highway authority prefers to acquire any land which is essential for highway drainage, so that is able to have control over the drainage infrastructure.

Highways across open land

While many of us may conjure a mental image of a rural Britain of sweeping country lanes bordered by high hedgerows, the fact is that most of our country roads are not bounded by hedges. In open country, highways are typically unmarked by either fence or hedge.

In the fens of eastern England, hundreds of miles of highways run along raised causeways with deep drainage channels on either side; here, the extent of the highway is fairly obvious. It extends only to the carriageway and the raised causeway on which it stands, while the drainage ditches are part of the farmland. For example, the A1101 runs for more than 50 miles, leading northwards from Bury St Edmonds, and yet it rarely rises above sea level. The fenland drainage ditches are part of the drainage system that forms the very fabric of the land, where 300,000 acres of prime farmland lie at or below sea level, rather than being part of highway infrastructure.

Elsewhere, upland roads will typically be open on both sides. Fencing will be used if livestock needs to be contained, but the boundaries of the highway itself will typically be unmarked. In such cases, the presumption is that the highway is just the surfaced carriageway. Anyone taking a drive through the Malvern Hills will notice that the carriageway tends to be unfenced, being entirely open to the countryside.

If the carriageway becomes impassable whether due to disrepair or periodic blockages such as seasonal mud or flooding, then the public has the right to deviate off the carriageway.

For this reason, many country lanes have very wide verges – before the road was surfaced, the highway would quickly become muddy and rutted, so carriages would divert to either side. These muddy spots would tend to be in the same place each Winter, and over the years parts of the highway network became very wide, while other parts remained the standard width. Those variations in width gradually crystallised into permanent features of the highway network.

These days, most of our highways have been surfaced and drained, so the problem of seasonal mud and flooding should be consigned to the history books. However, those very wide verges still remain, as a reminder that the right to use a highway includes a right to reasonable deviation in the event that the highway is blocked. The famous case of Dawes v Hawkins (of which more later) confirmed the long held principal that the public may deviate off the highway onto private land if the highway itself has become "foundrous or impassable". The adjoining landowners would surely be prompted to make an immediate call to the highway authority to sort the position out! Highway lawyers also have the unenviable task of explaining legal terms which have long passed out of common usage – with soil being lost from farmland in winter rain storms, many country lanes are in places ankle deep in mud during the winter, but we tend not to complain to our friends that the route was too foundrous!

Despite the right to deviate, please remember that the public does not have the right to meander. Any deviation must be limited to what is required to circumnavigate the obstruction.

Draining a highway

I have mentioned drainage several times already. Highways are often bounded by drainage ditches, which may belong to the neighbouring farmer, or may be part of the highway. Equally, they may be neither, being under the control of the Environment Agency as successor to special organisations such as the Bedford Levels Corporation that had started to maintain the extensive drainage ditch network in the Fens back in the 1600s.

The common law allows a landowner to drain rainwater onto the highway. As you might expect, such a right is in fact severely restrained. Given that a muddy carriageway may allow a highway user to deviate off the carriageway, it will come as no surprise that landowners must not allow mud to be carried onto the highway. Anyone travelling along a country lane in February will wonder how often this prohibition is ever enforced.

Landowners must not allow a footway to be waterlogged, for the protection of pedestrians.

Specifically, all landowners must take reasonable steps to abate the flow of water onto the highway. Drainage ditches must be kept clear and properly maintained. In urban areas, the rate of rainwater flow from front driveways onto the carriageway can cause real problems, as the Victorian storm drains will quickly overflow. Since 2008, anyone wishing to create a new hardstanding at the front of a house of more than five square metres, typically for the creation of a parking area in the place of a front garden, will need planning permission. One of the conditions imposed by the local planning authority is likely to be a drainage solution to try to direct rainwater into a soakaway or at least abate the flow from the driveway into the storm drains, but the use of a sump. From this, it follows that planning permission is not required if the hardstanding is designed to drain into a soakaway/sump within another part of your garden, or if the driveway is to be laid with porous blocks or gravel. As mentioned above, any gravel must be contained within the structure of the driveway so that it does not cause damage to the highway surface.

Homeowners should take note that it is an offence to allow rainwater to flow from the roof of a building onto persons passing below. For most of us, this can be prevented by the simple task of keeping guttering cleared and in decent repair. Perhaps more importantly, homeowners must take reasonable steps to prevent water from flowing over the footway or pavement of an adjoining highway.

Despite these conditions, the principal remains that landowners are allowed to drain onto the highway.

Conversely, the highway authority is not entitled to allow rainwater to flow from the highway onto surrounding land. Once the water is on the highway, the highway authority must deal with it. The highway authority must therefore take steps to ensure that the highway is properly drained, even if the water has come onto the highway from other neighbouring land.

In the case of **Bybrook Barn Garden Centre Limited v Kent County Council**, in 2000 (EWCA Civ 300), the Court of Appeal decided that the highway authority was liable for flooding from rainwater, because it had failed to upgrade the highway storm drains to keep pace with the increased flow of water caused by the development of surrounding land, alongside the motorway in Ashford, Kent. When the highway authority constructed the initial culvert, it was taking responsibility for the flow of natural water, and therefore had to keep on top of this problem. The culvert had been adequate when it was first constructed, but the increased flow of rainwater run-off due to the development of the M20 motorway and a nearby business park, meant that the highway authority should have upgraded its drains. The garden centre was flooded, and the highway authority was held liable; the flood waters did not come from a river, they were the product of overflowing highway drains. Even though the garden centre had been developed after the M20 motorway was built, the owner of the centre was entitled to be protected from the rainwater which flooded down from the motorway and the adjacent industrial and distribution parks. Presumably, the flooding was not repeated; the garden centre did relocate to a new site, but this is directly opposite, and even nearer to the M20 motorway. The old barn has been converted into a rather nice looking restaurant.

CHAPTER EIGHT
DOES A HIGHWAY LAST FOREVER?

I mentioned earlier that, once created, highway cannot be extinguished. As long ago as 1860, it was Mr Justice John Maynard Byles, while giving judgement in the leading case of Dawes v Hawkins, who seems to have been the first person to use the phrase "once a highway always a highway". His utterance has become a legal maxim. It is not possible to acquire ownership of a highway by adverse possession, as this would inevitably involve the committing of an offence of obstructing a highway. It is not possible for the owner of the subsoil of a highway simply to abandon it; the highway authority is required to keep all highways open for use by the public.

In July 1999 the Court of Appeal considered the case of Loder v Gaden and others (EWCA Civ 1998). The Court confirmed the old maxim, holding that if a claimant can show on the balance of probability that a highway existed hundreds of years ago, then the road is still a highway! In the case in question, the issue was not whether or not a highway had become lost (in the sense of being absorbed into a forest, or having buildings erected over it), but whether or not a road had ever been a highway at all.

The road in question was Sydenham Lane, near Broadwell in Gloucestershire. The Court awarded the defendant business an easement to use Sydenham Lane for the purpose of running its agricultural business, such that they could use the lane for lorries transporting cattle and sheep. Unfortunately for the defendants, this award was of very little use. The Gadens had been operating an agricultural haulage business from this rural location for the previous 18 years, storing and transporting straw, and intended to develop this side of the business on their land. The defendant had claimed that the road was a highway, despite being a narrow lane which only served the Gadens' farm and the land of their neighbours, the Loders.

The Gadens claimed that the road had been used as a highway for several centuries. The Court of Appeal disagreed, saying that it was merely a lane which served the Gadens' "insignificant pieces of pasture land." The defendant failed to persuade the Court that usage of the road was sufficient to claim that the road had been dedicated as a highway. On the evidence, the only users had been the Loders and the Gadens and their visitors, together with their respective predecessors in title. The Gadens failed to persuade the Court that the road had been an ancient highway used by the public at large. They did persuade the Court that there had been long user of the lane for agricultural purposes, which includes the moving of livestock, which is why they were awarded an easement. However, the storage of hay which was grown elsewhere is not "agriculture" so the easement would not be of any use for the Gadens' evolving and increasing requirements; the new easement allowed agriculture and the transporting of livestock or crops raised on the land, but not commercial haulage and distribution. The Court, presumably without a hint of irony, concluded that the Gadens were "clutching at straws". There had never been a highway.

While of no benefit to the Gadens, it was of great interest to lawyers that the Court of Appeal went on to state that had there been a highway hundreds of years ago, it would have still been a highway now. Once a highway, always a highway.

As we discussed earlier, the Natural Environment and Rural Communities Act 2006 was subsequently introduced in order to stop the public seeking to claim rights of highway over little-used ancient roads.

Can you extinguish a highway?

If a highway does exist, it is indeed possible to extinguish its status as a highway. This can be done in order to make the highway cease to exist altogether, or if you simply want to divert it to a new location. There are different procedures available in the Highways Act and also the Town and Country Planning Act 1990.

Whichever procedure you choose, you must first advertise your intention to stop up or divert, by way of press advertisement and also by posting notices at the side of the highway in question. Also, you must serve notices on all statutory undertakers, as they have the rights to lay services under the highway.

The highway authority make a stopping up order

If using the procedure in the Highways Act 1980, the process must be led by the highway authority, as it is the authority makes the stopping up order on the grounds that the highway is either unnecessary or can be diverted in order to make it "nearer or more commodious". Disputes may be referred to the Magistrates Court for an order.

While the highway authority may make such an order at its own behest, typically such orders are made following an application from a member of the public. Once an order is made, any party who has been detrimentally affected may claim compensation for the damage caused to land by the new highway or the associated construction works.

A highway may have become unnecessary if a new road is built, such as a town bypass, which renders the "old road" obsolete and un-used. The application for stopping up might be expected to be part of the development process for the new road, but equally it might only become apparent that the old road is no longer required some years after the completion of the new highway. Once stopped up the road ceases to be a highway, so reverts to its earlier status as a private road. The landowner can then redevelop the land, free from concerns about the highway status of the land.

The phrase "nearer or more commodious" does allow for the new route to be longer than the existing route, provided that it can be shown to be better and more convenient for the public.

If the highway in question is a footpath, the highway authority can seek a stopping up order if the footpath is not needed. Alternatively, the order may be sought because it is in the interests of the owner of the land that the footpath be diverted, provided that the start and end the footpath are not changed. A common example would be the diversion of a footpath to the margins of a field in order to allow for modern agricultural use of the field itself. In an urban setting, a footpath might be diverted in order to allow the valuable development of land. In either case, the start and end points are to remain unaltered.

What if a highway is preventing the implementation of a planning permission?

If the procedure set out in the Highways Act is not applicable, any member of the public may apply to the Secretary of State under section 247 of the Town and Country Planning Act 1990 for an order that the highway be stopped up or diverted in order that a planning permission may be carried out. A similar procedure is available under s257 TCCPA, for footpaths or bridleways only.

In other words, if the local planning authority has granted a planning permission which can only be implemented if a highway is diverted or stopped up, the landowner or developer may apply to the Secretary of State for an order for diversion or stopping up.

Equally, local planning authority has the right to make a stopping up or diversion order relating to footpaths and bridleways which are in the way of development for which planning permission has been granted.

A footpath can be "extinguished" by the Planning Inspectorate, if it is no longer needed, which is a strict test. By contrast, a footpath may be diverted if the new route is not substantially less convenient. Remember that the test under the Highways Act was that the footpath may be diverted if the new route is nearer or more commodious. The test under the Town and Country Planning Act 1990 is therefore slightly less strict than the Highways Act when it comes to diverting public footpaths.

What happens when a highway is stopped up?

Remember that the legal presumption is that the frontagers on either side of a highway each own the subsoil up to the mid-point, subject to the rights of highway over the surface. For those of you who like a bit of Latin, this may be referred to as the Ad Medium Filum presumption (literally "to the middle of the road"). As with all presumptions, there may well be evidence to the contrary.

If a highway is stopped up, or diverted, then the ownership of the subsoil becomes important. Once the highway has disappeared, the subsoil owner once again has full ownership of the land.

It is important to remember that there may well be services laid beneath the highway. Statutory utility companies will object to the application for stopping up, unless they are satisfied that their cables and pipes will be protected. The result will be that the landowner regains the land, free from the previous highway, but still has to maintain the safety of the underground services. Redevelopment is therefore impossible.

Utility companies will allow their services to be re-routed, but only if the new route is to their satisfaction and all works are carried out entirely at the landowner's cost. This may explain why a number of disused highways remain, having not been stopped up – the underground services lying beneath them render any stopping up somewhat pointless, as the land is still sterilised.

The presence of a gas main or public sewer beneath a road should be fairly easy to ascertain. However, private easements may be more difficult to spot. Once the highway is stopped up and the land effectively handed back to the subsoil owner, the rights of individuals which existed before the dedication as a highway become immediately revived. Private rights of way cannot be acquired by prescription while the road is a highway, but any such easements which had previously been acquired are brought back to life.

A landowner might cease to be the owner of a highway maintained by the council, but instead become the owner of a road which he or she must maintain at personal expense for the benefit of private users.

For this reason, modern deeds of easement may anticipate the fact that development cycles can often be short, with buildings erected and then demolished again just a few decades apart. The various deeds of easement may therefore be drafted to state that the private easement will cease if the road is ever dedicated as a highway, in order to prevent the easement being revived in the future, if and when the highway is stopped up.

CHAPTER NINE
CAN YOU OBSTRUCT A HIGHWAY?

It is an offence to obstruct a highway. This barely needs to be stated. However, highways are obstructed all the time, and many of us are responsible for this every day of our lives.

In local high streets, many shop keepers display their goods outside the front of their shops. Very often, the land immediately outside the shop is in fact a private forecourt, even if it is almost indistinguishable from the footway of the adopted highway. However, if the shopkeeper's goods stray onto the public footway, even if the local shops have done so for years, then this is actually an offence. It does not matter if the obstruction to the passing pedestrian is minor, it remains an offence. The local authority will tend to take a common sense approach, and only top prosecute as a last resort.

Parking a car on a highway is an obstruction but is not generally considered to be an offence because it is such a common occurrence. Car ownership is considered by many to be a fundamental aspiration for people in this country, and car owners want to have somewhere to park. From this, it follows that it is reasonable for motorists to be able to park their cars on the street outside their homes.to do. The Lord Chief Justice himself stated as long ago as 1956 that "no one is going to say that leaving a car for a reasonable time is an obstruction sufficient to make it an offence". It is therefore reasonable to park a car overnight outside your house.

It follows that the act of abandoning a car on the highway is an offence, as this is not considered reasonable. Some people use their cars every day, while other vehicles remain parked on the highway for weeks at a time. Presumably, it is lawful to park a car for long periods outside your home provided that it remains taxed. As mentioned earlier, vehicle excise duty (the tax disk, as people used to call it) is just a tax, and the funds raised have not been allocated to the repair of highways since the abolition of road tax in the 1930s, it is not lawful to place a vehicle on the highway unless the VED has been paid.

There is an inevitable grey area between a vehicle which has been parked in the long-term and one which has been abandoned, which itself partly depends on the level of inconvenience caused to other road users.

Equally, a car which is even briefly parked on a blind bend on an unlit road is a hazard to highway users, so the owner is likely to have committed an offence. How often do we see motorists attempting to avoid parking charges at countryside beauty spots by leaving their vehicles dangerously parked along narrow lanes, causing a hazard to everyone else? Occasionally, a traffic enforcement officer from the local police will arrive and issue penalty notices.

Parking on the verge or the footway is no more or less of an offence than parking on the carriageway, but the motorist is more likely to be causing an obstruction and is therefore more liable to prosecution. A parked vehicle that causes some temporary inconvenience to other vehicles is considered to be acceptable, but the traffic authority is less forgiving of parked vehicles which cause inconvenience to pedestrians. A blocked footway will force pedestrians, particularly those pushing prams or using mobility scooters, to divert onto the carriageway, where they are at greater danger from passing vehicles.

It is an offence to drive on a footway, subject to the common law right to be able to drive to and from your property which we discussed earlier. However, if you have parked your car on the pavement, you have presumably committed the offence of driving a vehicle on the footway. This particular point is rarely taken by the authorities, unless the motorist has driven a substantial distance along the footway.

Currently, in most of the country, the "half on-half off" method of parking on the pavement is deemed to be an acceptable compromise. Please note however that parking on the pavement (whether half on-half off or otherwise) has been illegal in London since 1974 under s15 of the Greater London Council (General Powers) Act 1974. Parking on the pavement will be illegal in Scotland from 2021 under s50 of the Transport (Scotland) Act 2019. Throughout the rest of the UK, regulations are left to local traffic authorities, but there is currently a consultation being carried out on the question of whether or not to make such parking illegal throughout England.

The commonsense approach applied to car owners is extended to people selling food from the highway. While shopkeepers are sometimes prosecuted for obstructing the footway, food vendors are generally only prosecuted if the stall is actually causing an obstruction to the footway, or if the stall appears to be permanent. Perhaps, the public's love of hot food is greater than its love of displays of hardware goods or fresh fruit? That said, it has been held to be an offence of obstruction to sell hot dogs from a van parked on the carriageway, even though the road in question was comfortably wide enough for this not to be a danger. The van was causing no more obstruction than a parked vehicle, but the Court clearly felt that the owner was acting unreasonably. Ice cream vans only stop temporarily in any location; if an ice cream seller took up a permanent pitch on the street, it would probably constitute an obstruction and therefore be an offence.

Scaffolding and skips will constitute an obstruction if placed on the highway, but the builder or homeowner can apply for a licence from highway authority. The equipment must be insured and properly lit, to avoid injury to passers-by. Permission will not be granted to place a skip on the footway, but scaffolding can be erected on the footway if necessary for building works. The responsibility lies with the property owner, but in many parts of the country the highway authority will accept an application from the skip/scaffolding contractor.

Gates – it is possible to put a gate on the highway without causing an "obstruction" provided that the gate is not locked. This is common in remote upland country areas, as a means of keeping livestock in their fields. The highway user simply has to stop, open the gate, pass through, and then close the gate again. Nobody thinks twice about this when using a rural public footpath, and the same principal applies to a vehicular highway.

Please note that it is an offence to obstruct a highway. If the gate cannot readily be opened, or is not serving any genuine purpose, then the owner of the gate may be held to have committed an offence.

Penalties for obstructing the highway

The penalty for obstructing the highway is a fine of up to £5,000 with a daily fine of £250 until the obstruction is removed. This applies whether the obstruction is an unwarranted gate, a badly parked car or a builder's skip.

CHAPTER TEN
A WORD ABOUT THE HIGHWAYS SEARCH

Highway status is not shown on Land Registry documents which are concerned only with ownership and not usage of land. Land Registry plans are drawn using Ordnance Survey mapping, which itself is only concerned by physical features and not by ownership. Therefore, a Land Registry plan does not confirm what land is used for and will contain many details and features which are entirely unconnected to the ownership of land.

Anyone purchasing or seeking to redevelop a property where there is any doubt whatsoever about the connection between the property in question and the nearby highway should carry out a Highways Search. This will show the highways in the vicinity of the search property. Section 36(6) of the Highways Act requires the highway authority to keep an up to date register of all highways maintainable at the public expense. It is important to submit your application with a plan which accurately shows the land in question, and also with a covering letter that explains the purpose of the search. If the applicant intends to redevelop the land, then the covering letter to the highway authority should state this fact.

In Chesterton Commercial (Oxon) v Oxfordshire County Council [2015 EGLR 62], the High Court held that a local authority was liable to a buyer for the loss in property value where a highway authority search result stated incorrectly that part of a property was not highway maintainable at public expense. The land in question had been bought for redevelopment, and the County Council was actively investigating the highway status of part of this land, which was to become a private car park following the redevelopment. The search result showed that the adopted highway abutted the property but omitted to mention that part of the property itself was potentially about to be included in the highway. The highway authority then concluded that a strip of the search property was indeed part of the adopted highway, in contradiction of the search result. The developer was therefore unable to create the required private car park, even though the search result was "clear".

The County Council had been told that the land was to be redeveloped, so was held liable for the developer's losses.

When reviewing a highways search result, remember to check the search result plan very carefully. If the boundary of the highway shown on the search result does not exactly match the boundaries used by the Land Registry, then there is a potential problem.

If there is a gap, then the gap might be deemed to be highway, or might be deemed to be part of the property. Remember the "hedge & ditch" and Ad Medium Filum presumptions which we discussed above. If the "gap land" can confidently be assumed to be part of the property, then there is nothing to worry about. However, most people are reluctant to rely on legal presumptions, particularly if large sums of development funding are about to be expended.

It may be that the Land Registry and the highway authority are using different maps, but unless one or other of them can be persuaded to update their mapping, the "gap" remains.

If the use of the land is not going to change, the landowner might be relaxed, and take the view that a satisfactory prescriptive easement will have been obtained across any gap land. However, if there is to be a change or use or an intensification, then any such prescriptive easement will be inadequate so the landowner may be required to negotiate with the highway authority for continued access to the property. This is likely to require some works to be carried out, which in turn will entail the landowner having to enter into an agreement under s278 of the Highways Act, as described above, in order to be able to continue using an established access point following a redevelopment.

Crucially, please remember that roads built by the council itself may not be listed, as any road built by a highway authority for the benefit of the public is a highway whether or not it is listed. Again, this will cause anxious moments for anyone about to purchase property which is to be accessed over such a road, particularly if records of who built the road, when and why are unavailable.

If the exact width of the highway is important, you must specifically raise this when commissioning the search – Gooden v Northants CC (2002, 1 EGLR Court of Appeal) which confirmed that the council is only required to provide information from the statutory list, unless a specific enquiry is made. If such an enquiry is made, then the council may well request a further fee for the carrying out of a non-standard search. In many cases, this will be money very well spent.

As we have discussed above, public footpaths are very frequently not adopted as maintainable at the public expense. They are simply paths or tracks crossing open ground. This difference is highlighted in the replies given by the council to a standard local authority search. There are two different questions: q2.1 enquires about highways maintainable at the public expense, while q2.2 asks about public rights of way, but without discussing whether or not the way is adopted. If a public footpath is adopted, it should be referred to in the reply to q2.1. If the footpath is only mentioned in response to enquiry q2.2, then the path may be assumed to be an unadopted pedestrian highway.

MORE BOOKS BY LAW BRIEF PUBLISHING

A selection of our other titles available now:-

'Covid-19, Homeworking and the Law – The Essential Guide to Employment and GDPR Issues' by Forbes Solicitors
'Covid-19, Force Majeure and Frustration of Contracts – The Essential Guide' by Keith Markham
'Covid-19 and Criminal Law – The Essential Guide' by Ramya Nagesh
'Covid-19 and Family Law in England and Wales – The Essential Guide' by Safda Mahmood
'Covid-19 and the Implications for Planning Law – The Essential Guide' by Bob Mc Geady & Meyric Lewis
'Covid-19, Residential Property, Equity Release and Enfranchisement – The Essential Guide' by Paul Sams and Louise Uphill
'Covid-19, Brexit and the Law of Commercial Leases – The Essential Guide' by Mark Shelton
'Covid-19 and the Law Relating to Food in the UK and Republic of Ireland – The Essential Guide' by Ian Thomas
'A Practical Guide to the General Data Protection Regulation (GDPR) – 2nd Edition' by Keith Markham
'Ellis on Credit Hire – Sixth Edition' by Aidan Ellis & Tim Kevan
'A Practical Guide to Working with Litigants in Person and McKenzie Friends in Family Cases' by Stuart Barlow
'Protecting Unregistered Brands: A Practical Guide to the Law of Passing Off' by Lorna Brazell
'A Practical Guide to Secondary Liability and Joint Enterprise Post-Jogee' by Joanne Cecil & James Mehigan

'A Practical Guide to the Pre-Action RTA Claims Protocol for Personal Injury Lawyers' by Antonia Ford
'A Practical Guide to Neighbour Disputes and the Law' by Alexander Walsh
'A Practical Guide to Forfeiture of Leases' by Mark Shelton
'A Practical Guide to Coercive Control for Legal Practitioners and Victims' by Rachel Horman
'A Practical Guide to Rights Over Airspace and Subsoil' by Daniel Gatty
'Tackling Disclosure in the Criminal Courts – A Practitioner's Guide' by Narita Bahra QC & Don Ramble
'A Practical Guide to the Law of Driverless Cars – Second Edition' by Alex Glassbrook, Emma Northey & Scarlett Milligan
'A Practical Guide to TOLATA Claims' by Greg Williams
'Artificial Intelligence – The Practical Legal Issues' by John Buyers
'A Practical Guide to the Law of Prescription in Scotland' by Andrew Foyle
'A Practical Guide to the Construction and Rectification of Wills and Trust Instruments' by Edward Hewitt
'A Practical Guide to the Law of Bullying and Harassment in the Workplace' by Philip Hyland
'How to Be a Freelance Solicitor: A Practical Guide to the SRA-Regulated Freelance Solicitor Model' by Paul Bennett
'A Practical Guide to Prison Injury Claims' by Malcolm Johnson
'A Practical Guide to the Small Claims Track' by Dominic Bright
'A Practical Guide to Advising Clients at the Police Station' by Colin Stephen McKeown-Beaumont
'A Practical Guide to Antisocial Behaviour Injunctions' by Iain Wightwick
'Practical Mediation: A Guide for Mediators, Advocates, Advisers, Lawyers, and Students in Civil, Commercial, Business, Property, Workplace, and Employment Cases' by Jonathan Dingle with John Sephton
'The Mini-Pupillage Workbook' by David Boyle

‘A Practical Guide to Crofting Law’ by Brian Inkster
‘A Practical Guide to Spousal Maintenance’ by Liz Cowell
‘A Practical Guide to the Law of Domain Names and Cybersquatting’ by Andrew Clemson
‘A Practical Guide to the Law of Gender Pay Gap Reporting’ by Harini Iyengar
‘A Practical Guide to the Rights of Grandparents in Children Proceedings’ by Stuart Barlow
‘NHS Whistleblowing and the Law’ by Joseph England
‘Employment Law and the Gig Economy’ by Nigel Mackay & Annie Powell
‘A Practical Guide to Noise Induced Hearing Loss (NIHL) Claims’ by Andrew Mckie, Ian Skeate, Gareth McAloon
‘An Introduction to Beauty Negligence Claims – A Practical Guide for the Personal Injury Practitioner’ by Greg Almond
‘Intercompany Agreements for Transfer Pricing Compliance’ by Paul Sutton
‘Zen and the Art of Mediation’ by Martin Plowman
‘A Practical Guide to the SRA Principles, Individual and Law Firm Codes of Conduct 2019 – What Every Law Firm Needs to Know’ by Paul Bennett
‘A Practical Guide to Adoption for Family Lawyers’ by Graham Pegg
‘A Practical Guide to Industrial Disease Claims’ by Andrew Mckie & Ian Skeate
‘A Practical Guide to Redundancy’ by Philip Hyland
‘A Practical Guide to Vicarious Liability’ by Mariel Irvine
‘A Practical Guide to Applications for Landlord’s Consent and Variation of Leases’ by Mark Shelton
‘A Practical Guide to Relief from Sanctions Post-Mitchell and Denton’ by Peter Causton
‘A Practical Guide to Equity Release for Advisors’ by Paul Sams
‘A Practical Guide to Unlawful Eviction and Harassment’ by Stephanie Lovegrove
‘A Practical Guide to the Law Relating to Food’ by Ian Thomas

'A Practical Guide to Financial Services Claims' by Chris Hegarty

'The Law of Houses in Multiple Occupation: A Practical Guide to HMO Proceedings' by Julian Hunt

'A Practical Guide to Unlawful Eviction and Harassment' by Stephanie Lovegrove

'A Practical Guide to Solicitor and Client Costs' by Robin Dunne

'Occupiers, Highways and Defective Premises Claims: A Practical Guide Post-Jackson – 2nd Edition' by Andrew Mckie

'A Practical Guide to Financial Ombudsman Service Claims' by Adam Temple & Robert Scrivenor

'A Practical Guide to Advising Schools on Employment Law' by Jonathan Holden

'A Practical Guide to Running Housing Disrepair and Cavity Wall Claims: 2nd Edition' by Andrew Mckie & Ian Skeate

'A Practical Guide to Holiday Sickness Claims – 2nd Edition' by Andrew Mckie & Ian Skeate

'Arguments and Tactics for Personal Injury and Clinical Negligence Claims' by Dorian Williams

'A Practical Guide to QOCS and Fundamental Dishonesty' by James Bentley

'A Practical Guide to Drone Law' by Rufus Ballaster, Andrew Firman, Eleanor Clot

'A Practical Guide to Compliance for Personal Injury Firms Working With Claims Management Companies' by Paul Bennett

'A Practical Guide to the Landlord and Tenant Act 1954: Commercial Tenancies' by Richard Hayes & David Sawtell

'A Practical Guide to Dog Law for Owners and Others' by Andrea Pitt

'RTA Allegations of Fraud in a Post-Jackson Era: The Handbook – 2nd Edition' by Andrew Mckie

'RTA Personal Injury Claims: A Practical Guide Post-Jackson' by Andrew Mckie

'On Experts: CPR35 for Lawyers and Experts' by David Boyle

'An Introduction to Personal Injury Law' by David Boyle

'A Practical Guide to Chronic Pain Claims' by Pankaj Madan
'A Practical Guide to Claims Arising from Fatal Accidents' by James Patience
'A Practical Guide to Subtle Brain Injury Claims' by Pankaj Madan

www.ingramcontent.com/pod-product-compliance
Lightning Source LLC
LaVergne TN
LVHW022308200926
848481LV00004B/1241